D0116513

We Go!

Boats

Dana Meachen Rau

Marshall Cavendish
Benchmark
New York

We go in a boat.

Boats go on water.

Boats go in wind.

7

Boats go with a paddle.

Boats go with gas.

Boats hold people.

Boats hold cars.

Boats hold life vests.

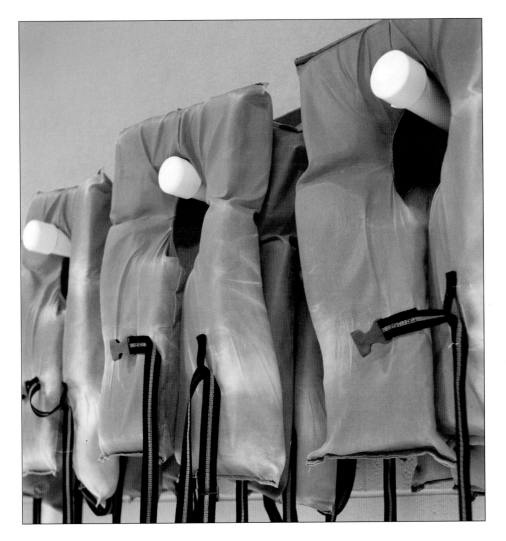

We go in a boat!

19

Words to Know

cars

gas

life vests

paddle

people

water

wind

Index

Page numbers in **boldface** are illustrations.

cars, 14, **15**, **20**

gas, 10, **11**, **20**

life vests, **3**, **9**, 16, **17**, **20**

paddle, **3**, 8, **9**, **20**
people, **3**, **5**, **7**, **9**, 12, **13**, **19**, **21**

water, 4, **5**, **21**
wind, 6, **7**, **21**

About the Author

Dana Meachen Rau is the author of many other titles in the Bookworms series, as well as other nonfiction and early reader books. She lives in Burlington, Connecticut, with her husband and two children.

With thanks to the Reading Consultants:

Nanci Vargus, Ed.D., is an Assistant Professor of Elementary Education at the University of Indianapolis.

Beth Walker Gambro is an Adjunct Professor at the University of Saint Francis in Joliet, Illinois.

Marshall Cavendish Benchmark
99 White Plains Road
Tarrytown, New York 10591-9001
www.marshallcavendish.us

Text copyright © 2010 by Marshall Cavendish Corporation

Library of Congress Cataloging-in-Publication Data

Rau, Dana Meachen, 1971-
Boats / by Dana Meachen Rau.
p. cm. — (Bookworms. We go!)
Includes index.
Summary: "Describes the physical attributes, different kinds, and purposes of boats"—Provided by publisher.
ISBN 978-0-7614-4076-5
1. Boats and boating—Juvenile literature. I. Title.
VM150.R37 2009
623.82—dc22
2008042500

Editor: Christina Gardeski
Publisher: Michelle Bisson
Designer: Virginia Pope
Art Director: Anahid Hamparian

Photo Research by Anne Burns Images

Cover Photo by *Alamy Images*/Bill Bachmann

The photographs in this book are used with permission and through the courtesy of:
Corbis: pp. 1, 7, 21B Onne van der Wal; p. 3 Ariel Skelley; pp. 9, 20BR Larry Williams/zefa; pp. 13, 21TL David Sailors;
pp. 15, 20TL Walter Bibikow; p. 19 Neil Rabinowitz. *Photo Edit, Inc.*: pp. 5, 21TR Tony Freeman.
iStock: pp. 11, 20TR Elena Vdovina; pp. 17, 20BL iStock.

Printed in Malaysia
1 3 5 6 4 2